W9-BJQ-163

COMBAT
HELICOPTERS

COMBAT
HELICOPTERS

JERRY SCUTTS

**MALLARD
PRESS**

MALLARD PRESS

MALLARD PRESS
An imprint of BDD Promotional Book Company Inc.
666 Fifth Avenue, New York, NY 10103

Mallard Press and its accompanying design and logo
are trademarks of BDD Promotional Book Company

First published in the United States of America in 1989
by The Mallard Press

First published in Great Britain in 1989 by the
Hamlyn Publishing Group, Michelin House,
81 Fulham Road, London SW3 6RB

ISBN 0-792-450-14-0

Printed and bound in Spain by Gráficas Estella, S.A. Navarra.

Contents

Jolly Green Giants

Below: The Sikorsky R-4 first flew in 1939. Four years later US Coast Guard flyers used the HNS-1 to prove the concept of rotary-winged operations at sea. On 30 October 1943 a float-equipped machine made the first public flight from a ship.

If armed conflict should ever break out between nations equipped with modern state-of-the-art helicopters, it would not be too long before such machines clashed over the battlefield and attempted to shoot each other down, probably using air-to-air missiles. Heliborne hardware, thoroughly tested in the 1950s, had

its baptism of fire in Vietnam and has since matured into weaponry very much to be reckoned within the tactical combat scenario of the 1990s.

Of all the nations that now employ helicopters in a military role – and there are very few which do not – the United States has enjoyed an enviable lead. Along with the Soviet Union, which very quickly saw the potential of the vertical lifting aircraft to traverse its own vast territory and developed its own designs, many of which remain unique, the US grasped this new regime of flight very quickly. Along with Germany and Britain, the US had developed rotorcraft suitable for military purposes before the end of World War II and soon afterward became the single most important production source of viable helicopters.

By the early 1950s the design team led by Igor Sikorsky had established machines such as the R-5 and H-19 in the inventories of US armed forces, and it was with the latter that the Army first began experiments to arm the helicopter so that it might fulfill a greater front line role than hitherto.

With the creation of the Air Force in 1947, the US Army began a long fight far away from any battlefield, to own and operate its own aviation assets, particularly for direct support

of troops in the field. The Marine Corps faced something of the same problem, although it had long enjoyed its own autonomous air cover, but here the problem was adequate funding. For the Army, aviation assets hinged on the helicopter. The potential of these versatile machines was enough to make the humble truck obsolete as a troop transport and by the end of the Korean War helicopters and proved to be invaluable for this and other duties, particularly that of casualty evacuation.

The Troop Lift Role

After Korea the Army and Marine Corps gradually developed their inventories of helicopters, primarily for the troop lift role. Still Sikorsky led the field, designs such as the H-34 which retained many features of the larg-

The H-19 was used widely by the USAF, primarily for rescue work with the Military Air Transport service, designated SH-19.

7

Above: Workhorse of the US Army, the H-34 Choctaw first entered service in 1955 to become one of the most successful helos of all time.

Opposite: First tandem-rotor helo in Air Force service, the H-21 was also an early rescue type. The machine seen here is using water-landing pontoons.

er H-19 and H-37 entering service during the 1950s. During this period Piasecki (later Vertol) entered the picture with the H-21, known as the Shawnee by the US Army, and Bell's tiny H-13 Sioux provided a helicopter able to undertake a wide variety of roles, including training and casevac.

Equipped with helicopter designs capable of putting a sizeable force in the field in minimum time and to keep it supplied with supplies and ammunition, remove casulaties and insert fresh troops, the US Army entered the 1960s as well endowed with its own aviation as any comparable military organisation in the Western world. Then came the first signs of

unrest in South East Asia. The US, pledged to assist friendly powers under threat in the region, began sending 'advisors' to enable indigenous forces to defend themselves, using largely American methods and arms.

Slowly, the war in Vietnam spread with the result that US helicopters, flying troop-carrying missions for government forces, began to be fired upon. It was at that point that the US Army embarked on studies that were to lead to heated exchanges with the Air Force over the whole future of organic aviation. Those studies sought to arm helicopters.

A logical-enough desire in the circumstances, the very thought of Army helicopters carrying armament systems and defending themselves, was seen in USAF circles as a challenge to the fundamental and traditional role of the Air Force to provide close air support to troops in the field. Things came to a head when the Army put forward a case for having its own fixed-wing troop transports, based on the Canadian DHC-7 Caribou.

A trade-off was arranged whereby the Army could keep its helicopter force, armed or otherwise, while the Air Force would retain the troop carrier role, short of actual battle-field support – which was anyway being overtaken by helicopters. In the long run, this arrangement suited the Army because it obtained funding for thousands of helicopters in all categories, far more than it might otherwise have been allowed. It is, however, interesting

to speculate what the modern US Army might have become considering that there were programmes developed in the 1960s designed to prove a case for that service operating its own fixed-wing close support aircraft if armed helicopters had not proven successful. Among the aircraft tested for such roles were the Fiat G.91 and Northrop F-5.

But the gestation period of the armed helicopter (or more accurately, the 'dedicated' helicopter gunship) was fraught with diffi-

Below: Progressive updates in Chinook capability led to the CH-47D, one of which is seen here awaiting its air show slot.

culties. Much deliberation at the highest levels attended the reports of tests using helicopters already in inventory. Fortunately, the right helicopter was waiting, for in February 1955 the Army had awarded Bell a contract for a new utility helicopter. Flying as the XH-40 in October 1956 the Bell design was powered by a compact gas turbine engine, a revolutionary step forward for a service helicopter, offering as it did greater reliability, more power and simpler drive systems than is possible with

piston engines. Above all, the horizontal 'cabin roof' mounting of the Bell design allowed the maximum cabin space for the carriage of troops and supplies. Army orders were placed early in March 1959 and in the spring of that year Bell's Forth Worth plant began producing the UH-1 – the 'Huey' was born.

Gas Turbines

Immediately prior to its ever deeper involvement in the Vietnam conflict, the US Army also ordered other helicopters which were to stand it in good stead in both war and peace for decades to come. The 'new generation' gas turbine helicopters emerged to fill the multiplicity of roles undertaken by older

Bell UH-1B

Powerplant: 1 × 960 shp Lycoming T53-L-5 shaft turbine

Dimensions: main rotor diameter 44 ft; fuselage length 39 ft 7$\frac{1}{2}$ in; height 14 ft 7 in

Weights: (empty) 4,502 lb; Max T/O weight 8,500 lb

Performance: economic cruise 126 mph; rate of climb at S/L 2,350 ft/min; range: 253 miles with 800 lb payload

Above: Bell's 1955 utility design sold well abroad. This Agusta-Bell AB-204B is part of the 3rd Helicopter Wing, Austrian Air Force.

Following page:
Hughes' diminutive OH-6 Cayuse took its more popular name 'Loach' from its type designation – Light Observation. Working with gunships the OH-6 aero scout platoons shouldered one of the most dangerous jobs in Vietnam, the enemy exacting a fearful toll to mask their activity from prying eyes of Loach crews.

piston-engined types and give the Army a far greater flexibility, enabling it to develop the 'air mobile' concept to the full.

With the UH-1 ready to fill the broadly interpreted 'utility' role, the Army also selected a new heavy lift helicopter in the shape of the Boeing Vertol CH-47 Chinook. By their very nature helicopters are adaptable, not only to different roles to meet the needs of one service, but to be equally useful to another. So it was that the Chinook, selected by the Army in March 1959, was based on the Marines' CH-46 Sea Knight. Considerably larger than its younger stablemate, the CH-47 was designed to carry up to 40 fully equipped troops or a useful internal load of freight, with further outside loads being slung under the fuselage from a cargo hook.

Huge by Western standards, the Chinook's maximum weight was 46,000 lb, significantly more than the 31,000 lb gross of the H-37, previously the largest helicopter the Army had ordered. Some five years after placing the first CH-47 order, the Army acquired the even larger but more specialised CH-54 Tarhe or Skycrane. Longer than two UH-1Bs, the gawky Tarhe was an interesting approach to the big lift task; lacking an integral cabin it relied solely on slung loads or could accommodate a purpose-built removable pod which was suspended below the slim fuselage.

At the other end of the weight scale was the light observation helicopter. Under a design

competition initiated in 1960 the Army chose the Hughes (since 1984 a subsidiary of McDonnell Douglas) submission, the 2,700-lb H-6 Cayuse. One of the smallest helicopters ever developed for military use the H-6 – or OH-6 as it was originally known under the tri-

Above: A CH-46 Sea Knight disembarks its crew on USS Iwo Jima.

13

service designation system introduced in 1962 – was initially unarmed. But experience in Vietnam proved that even a little guy can pack a healthy punch, so during and after the war the Hughes 'Loach' came with a fearsome armament array. Each type of helicopter tended to have its own armament sub-system or range of systems fitted if it was expected to spend time in combat zones on duties other than casevac or rescue.

Guns for the Huey

In a war with a known front line, helicopters could re-supply positions from relatively safe areas in the rear of the action, as often occurred in Korea. But in Vietnam where there were no clearly defined lines, the problem of troop insertion, extraction and re-supply took on an entirely new dimension. While areas were nominally cleared as 'cold' landing zones (meaning that little or no opposition was expected) the situation could change rapidly. By the time the heliborne force arrived, the selected landing zones could have turned very 'hot' indeed, and it was for this reason that the Army instigated extensive research into the best ways to protect troop landings from the air. The early field tests were largely built aroung the H-34, which began to equip Army units in April 1955. Armament tests began the following year with what was rapidly becoming the Army's most numerous helicopter type.

Most standard weapons of the period were fitted and fired from the H-34s used in the tests, including .30 and .50 in MGs, 20 mm cannon, multiple 2.5 in folding-fin rockets launched from separate tubes, Tiny Tim rockets and Bullpup air-to-ground missiles. Often jury-rigged on field-constructed metal platforms and racks with multiple support bars, these offensive loads were only a step along the way. They provided useful data and proved that you could indeed use fixed guns and stand-off ordnance from a helicopter-borne platform with reasonable accuracy. But the configuration of the H-34 and other piston-engined helicopters did not allow much space for more equipment and it was not until the advent of the UH-1 that manufacturers such as Emerson and General Electric were able to put their long expertise in the armament business to practical use in new custom-designed systems tailored specifically to the Bell helicopter.

Development work continued as the first UH-1 deployed to Vietnam in April 1962, much useful information being fed back to the manufactuers of armament by the machines that followed in September of that year. These Hueys were operated by the Utility Tactical Transport Company, whose job it was to fly actual combat missions using their aircraft to escort troop-carrying helicopters, report on the results of using helicopter weapons and to suggest improvements.

Opposite: Well over 100 troops could be landed by this type of mass lift by UH-1Hs, the updated Delta model of the famed Huey.

Modern Armed Helicopters

Opposite: Fully-laden UH-1Ds of the 229th Assault Helicopter Battalion lift off for another Vietnam mission. 'B' and 'C' Company machines used the blue square and circle respectively.

Below: In more peaceful skies, a UH-1B makes an Army delivery flight.

So far as deployment is concerned, the story of the modern armed helicopter can be dated from 9 October 1962. That day UTTHCO's UH-1As flew as part of Operation 'Morning Star', one of thousands of operations flown into the military regions of South Vietnam with the primary object of finding and destroying NVA or VC forces. Often they were boosted in resources and scope and, before 1965, were conducted largely by the South Vietnamese Army which, in the early days at least, had numerous problems, not the least of which was understanding the full potential and versatility of helicopters.

On 20 November 1962 UTTHCO received the first UH-1Bs, more powerful than the A model and armed with the first custom-designed weapons systems. A vast improvement over the fixed MG and rocket tube arrangements fitted to the UH-1A, pilots now had a flexible, quad MG kit consisting of twin M-60C MGs on stub mountings each side of the

UNITED STATES ARMY

Huey. Fired by a special cabin sight, the guns had a maximum range of 750 yards.

Monitored by Army Concept Team in Vietnam, UTTHCO's armed helicopter experiment lasted until 15 March 1963. In that period pilots and crews worked out procedures that would become standard in the years to come; under the rules of engagement then prevailing the armed Hueys could not initiate fire, responding only when fired upon. But the concept was a success – armed helicopter escorts cut troop transport casualties by 25%.

As the US involvement in Vietnam intensified to reach a peak by 1966 the insert-attack-pull-back strategy for infantry assualts continued and led to mounting enemy casualties. Armed helicopters helped reduce US casualties to a minimum, rapidly becoming an integral part of Army operations.

But while air mobility could exact a fearful toll on insurgent forces the enemy was far from defenseless, even though the NVA/VC had no air cover. Combat troops in South Vietnam built a formidable local defense against helicopters, using everything from small arms to anti-aircraft MG. They learned the vulnerable points of each US helicopter and became adept at inflicting damage during the vulnerable landing and take off phases of assault landings. One big advantage the defenders enjoyed was that they could hear a helicopter assault coming, thereby reducing the risk of being surprised and there was often

ample time to prepare a hot reception.

The US Army could do little about the noise its helicopters made and the distinctive whistling 'whump, whump, whump' of the UH-1 was one of the most distinctive sound effects of the war.

The best form of defense in the South East Asian war was found to be attack; by an overwhelming use of firepower in the troop assault areas the Army reduced casualties and achieved a high kill rate among enemy forces. But sometimes the heavily armed UH-1B and C gunships had difficulties in keeping up with the lighter troop-carrying helicopters, especially in the predominant 'hot and high' conditions of the battle zone. With their own defensive armament of two M-60 door guns, the Huey 'slicks' were able to deal with localised ground fire and when it came to a heavier attack the gunships proved their worth. But it became apparent that if a faster helicopter was available, better tailored to the attack task, then air mobility would be that much more versatile.

The statistics of combat were the object of detailed analysis by service chiefs and industry and when in late 1964 the Army circulated its requirement for a high-performance helicopter gunship, the response was encouraging. Contractors knew that a winning proposal under the Advanced Aerial Fire Support System was bound to involve many airframes worth hundreds of thousands of dollars. At the

same time, building such a machine from scratch was no easy task.

Bell Helicopter, building on experience gained with its UH-1 series, consolidated its advantage and looked again at the Iroquois Warrior, or Sioux Scout as it became known. Based on an OH-13 airframe to cut costs, this little machine featured a completely new fuselage with the crew seated in tandem under a 'bubble' canopy. The Scout had stub wings mounted below the rotor and a tail rotor and main transmission borrowed from the commercial Model 47. Most distinctive of all was the large nose turret mounting two M-60 MGs.

Dedicated Gunships

Bell flight-tested the Scout extensively and proved that the dedicated gunship helicopter was a viable proposition. The company was therefore well placed to enter the AAFSS competition – which it in fact lost to rival designs from Lockheed and Sikorsky. The reason was not untypical; the Army was in effect attempting to jump a generation and procure a highly sophisticated 'de luxe' gunship helicopter long before the concept had proved its worth. It became clear that development of either the Lockheed AH-56 Cheyenne or Sikorsky S-66 Blackhawk would have taken much longer than was desired; cost was also a factor.

Undaunted by the decision of AAFSS, Bell decided to press ahead with a prototype of a refined Scout, incorporating many features of the experimental machine. Among the features Bell and the Army found desirable were the stepped tandem cockpit, the rotor system as used on the UH-1 and the turret gun. Mating these to an airframe utilising as many UH-1 components as possible would, it was estimated, create a gunship in the shortest possible time. Deployment to Vietnam could then be made in time for the new type to have some effect on operations.

By 7 September 1965 Bell had made the first flight of the Model 209 and after extensive testing the Army placed the first orders in April 1966. Initially known as the UH-1H, the suffix letter was changed to G and the new gunship became the HueyCobra, with an appropriate 'attack' rather than 'utility' prefix. Ordered as a stopgap pending something else, the HueyCobra was not alone in aviation history by becoming successful in its own right. And as had happened before, the hoped-for aircraft failed to materialise, leaving the field clear for the world's first attack helicopter to find its niche and be developed well beyond its original design expectation. As with its older stablemate, the 'Cobra grew, both in power and capability.

Largely combatting a non-mechanised enemy in SE Asia, the HueyCobra became the US Army's principal anti-tank (AT) helicopter in the period immediately following American withdrawal from that theater. Once the principles of AT warfare using helicopters had

Opposite: Bell's air to air photographer captures a UH-1D en route to its largest customer.

The twin-engined UH-1N was ordered by USAF for various duties including the all-important training role. The example seen here is from the 1550th Aircrew Training and Test Wing at Kirtland AFB, New Mexico.

been established toward the end of the Vietnam War by the UH-1, and AG-1, the Cobra rapidly took over the role, using a Hughes missile developed for that specific use. It would share the Army's anti-armor duty with the second gunship type to enter service, the Hughes AH-64 Apache.

HueyCobra Development

It was the US Marine Corps which was instrumental in pushing ahead with the development of a twin-engined HueyCobra after the Corps had successfully evaluated the single-engined 'Cobra starting in April 1969. Useful

though the attack helicopter was seen to be, the Marines wanted the added reliability of twin engines, and although Bell had few problems in adapting the airframe to accommodate a military version of the 1,800 shp T400 Twin Pac built by United Aircraft of Canada, the Marines thought procurement might stretch their budget more than a little. In the event, Vietnam attrition of UH-1 helicopters soon enabled the Corps to replace these utility helicopters with the AH-1J SeaCobra. By replacing losses and obtaining Department of Defense support for the program, the first SeaCobra was ready by October 1969. After a full evaluation, the AH-1J was despatched to Vietnam in February 1971. By late April the combat test period had revealed that the AH-1J was significantly more effective than the AH-1G.

With procurement thus assured, the Marines formed the first attack helicopter unit, HMS-269; flying UH-1s pending the delivery of enough Sea Cobras, the unit was officially commissioned on 1 July 1970.

Although the Marines' order for the AH-1J reached 124 examples during 1970, not all of them were delivered – at least not as standard machines. As with the Army, the Marines recognised the importance of AT capability and the advent of the TOW missile resulted in some significant changes in the configuration. Being a heavier machine than the AH-1G, the SeaCobra required uprated engines in order

to carry TOW, associated armor for its intended battlefield role, plus IR suppressors, jamming equipment and decoys. More powerful engines also required a larger rotor and gradually the new Marine Cobra grew both in size and weight.

Incorporating the necessary changes, Bell flew the first improved SeaCobra as the AH-1T in June 1976. The principal difference was in fuselage length compared with the AH-1J, but the rotor blades were longer, sweeping a 48 ft diameter and the tail rotor was repositioned

Above: Low over friendly jungle, a Marine crew tests the prototype AH-1T, which compared with the AH-1J has a lengthened fuselage and other changes.

Above: Thoroughly sold on the helicopter gunship during Vietnam combat, the Marines have across the board capability in composite squadrons which are primarily composed of helicopters such as the AH-1T shown above, on up to the fixed-wing AV-8 Harriers. As always, the job is to protect the 'mud Marines' slogging it out on the ground.

on top of the fin instead of being fin-side mounted as in all other Cobra models.

The P&W T400-WV-402 Twin Pack engine gave 1,970 shp for take-off, the AH-1T tipping the scales at 14,000 lb – some 4,000 lb more than the HueyCobra. Being larger and heavier, the improved SeaCobra could also deliver more ordnance. The stub wings could take four TOW tubes per side plus a range of other stores, depending on mission requirements.

Thus configured, the AH-1T had a maximum speed of 180 kt and could cruise at up to 142 kt; standard fuel load offered a range of 311 nm with a 3,327 lb payload and the aircraft had a service ceiling of 12,450 ft. Having accepted over 50 improved SeaCobras the Marines planned for a further update of the design, which would emerge, first as the AH-1T + SuperCobra and subsequently under the

more convenient designation AH-1W. The name SuperCobra was retained.

Based around the General Electric T700 Twin Pack which boosted power to 3,340 shp, the latest sea-going Cobra's primary armament is the potent Rockwell Hellfire laser-guided anti-armor missile, which has about twice the range of TOW and other similar role AGMs. The advantage of Hellfire is its ability to hit the target from both low and high level trajectories, the latter requiring remote designation from the launch helicopter. Each SuperCobra carries eight missiles.

The Marines ordered 44 AH-1Ws in 1985 and confirmed that a further 50 would be acquired by modernisation of AH-1T airframes after delivery of new aircraft was complete. The first AH-1W was delivered in March 1986.

Army Cobras for the 1990s

While the Marines went for a twin-engined Cobra, the Army elected to stay with the single-engine configuration. After the withdrawal from South East Asia the Army, too, concentrated on a primary anti-armor role for its sizeable helicopter gunship force. Briefly re-examining the moribund AAFSS designs it was decided instead to concentrate on an update program for the AH-1G to bring it up to modern battlefield standard. Having procured over 1,000 HueyCobras by 1972 the Army worked with Bell to incorporate new systems and weaponry for future service of the type, much information being determined by test data from the two Bell KingCobras, design studies which although not entering production, served to link the AH-1G and the 'navalised' AH-1J/W.

In January 1974, the Army ordered a modification program which would bring 101 AH-

Below: To distinguish the improved AH-1W from other Marine Cobras, Bell hung a 'Super' prefix and a slick black and gold paint scheme on the first machines. Note the measuring instrumented probe under the laser snout.

1Gs up to AH-1Q standard, fully capable of launching TOW missiles. Under a wide-ranging, multi-phase procurement, the Army eventually received the sophisticated AH-1S Modernised Cobra with AT and close support/escort capability, the rebuilding program taking about ten years. After the AH-1Q conversions came several hundred re-engined AH-1S Modified Cobras which differed from the original by having flat panel canopy sections and a laser designator in the extreme nose.

Production AH-1S models were TOW compatible from the start, in turn being upgraded as Modernised Cobras and these, the last examples of the HueyCobra design to be operated by the US Army, will remain in service through the early part of the next century. A further upgrading, with Hughes C-NITE night attack system is expected to extend service life for the decade 1995–2005.

Despatching two rounds of bad news to hostile tank commanders, an AH-1S crew practises for the real thing over a TOW test range.

Navy and Marine Hueys

Whereas the Marine Corps operated both the UH-1 and AH-1 in attack, transport, training and support roles, the US Navy was an early convert to the gunship concept, as exemplified by the armed Huey. That service was to remain with the 'utility' version and did not acquire Cobras, although Vietnam involvement was to create a whole new operational arena when Navy UH-1s flew in support of an unusual waterborne force within the waterways of South Vietnam. Protecting the 'brown water Navy' became the task of the famed Seawolves, the UH-1 force created in 1966.

Operating from LSTs stationed at different

Left: The Navy's version of the early Huey was the Lima model. This view shows how Bell's rotor balance bar rotated with the main blades.

Right: The Air Force ordered the UH-1H primarily for liaison and general utility work. This H model is a rescue ship and judging by their urgency, the crew has just received a call to action.

points on the Mekong River Delta waterways, these Hueys turned in an impressive record, 'writing the book' as they went. Among the many different types of mission flown were those at night, a hazardous and demanding business. But the success of nocturnal helicopter operations meant that Navy patrol boats could operate around the clock. Night formation flying with a difference was a Seawolves' speciality.

After a sundown briefing on known enemy activity and whereabouts, a two-ship UH-1 element would lift off, the lead helicopter flying typically at 500 ft with rotating beacon and navigation lights illuminated. This apparently dangerous light show masked the fact that the second Huey was above the leader, completely blacked out. Should the enemy be tempted to open fire on the leader, the invisible machine would drop into the target area with devastating results.

Towards the end of the US involvement, the Seawolves got a small number of UH-1Ls and further quantities of armed Hueys. The former was a training and utility version of the UH-1 with an uprated engine, and the Navy subsequently operated the HH-1K in the air-sea rescue role. When the Seawolves, alias Helicopter Attack (Light) Squadron Three (HA(L)-3) decommissioned on 26 January 1972, a unique US Navy unit ended an unusual chapter in the annals of helicopter operations and the history of that force.

The Navy's Seasprite

The US Navy's 'own' helicopter type of the Vietnam war period was the Kaman UH-2 Seasprite. Originating from a design competition set in 1956 for a high-performance, all-weather helicopter able to undertake a variety of tasks, particularly round-the-clock planeguard missions from aircraft carriers, the Kaman proposal was then known as the HU2K. The company won the competition and the prototype first flight was made on 2 July 1959.

Seasprite deliveries began in December 1962, the first two units to operate it being HC-1 and -2 and these squadrons deployed detachments aboard ships of the Pacific and Atlantic fleets respectively. Initially designated HU-2A, the Seasprite line developed with the UH-2B, although this variant, which had simpler equipment for VFR-only operations, was subsequently modified to the full-IFR capability similar to the UH-2A.

But the most significant improvement made to the Seasprite was to give it the added safety factor of twin engines. Both the UH-2A and -B had a single GE T58-GE-8 offering 1,250 shp but in March 1965 Kaman completed the first of two examples of the UH-2Bs with one T58-GE-8B engine in pod mounts on both sides of the main rotor housing. With additional alterations to the cockpit and rotor pylon, plus some increase in tail area the twin Seasprite became the UH-2C. Of the original order for 190 UH-2s,

Opposite: Ticking over on the fantail of the frigate Oliver Hazard Perry, a YSH-2G Seasprite is prepared for lift off in June 1985. It belongs to one of three Naval Reserve Force squadrons which supply LAMPS-1 helicopters to other ships.

Kaman SH-2 Seasprite

Powerplant: 2 × 1,350 shp General Electric T58 free turbine turboshafts

Dimensions: main rotor diameter 44 ft; fuselage length 40 ft 6 in; height 13 ft 7 in

Weights: empty 6,953 lb; max loaded 13,300 lb

Performance: Max speed 168 mph; max climb rate 2,440 ft/min; ceiling 22,500 ft; range 422 miles

Festooned Seasprite presents quite a headache for hostile submariners should its detection gear and offensive load ever be called upon for use 'in anger'.

40 conversions were made. Six examples, redesignated HH-2C, were converted to gunship configuration with a nose-turret-mounted 7.62 mm Minigun and two similar weapons as flexible doors guns. These machines also had dual mainwheels, a four-bladed tail rotor, an uprated transmission and armor protection.

Operated in the vital but highly dangerous Combat SAR role, armed and unarmed Seasprites effected many daring rescues during the Vietnam War, such as that on the night of 19 June 1968. Lifting off from his parent ship, USS *Preble* (DLG-15), Lt (*jg*) Clyde Lassen of HC-7 headed his UH-2A into North Vietnam to pick up the downed crew of an F-4 Phantom. Arriving at the point of pick up and dropping flares, the Seasprite came under enemy fire. It hit a tree after the flares burned out and Lassen had difficulty keeping the helo under control. Another flare drop failed to get the crew aboard and Lassen took the extreme risk of switching on his landing lights. His aircraft a beacon for enemy fire, Lassen nevertheless completed the rescue without harm to his crew. Back on board the *Jouett* (DLG-29) the Seasprite had fuel for five minutes more flying.

Along with the Seasprite, the Navy made extensive use of the Sikorsky Sea King to rescue shot-down airmen out of North Vietnam. A rugged, widely used type, the H-3 series of medium helicopters fathered an entire family of helicopters which were to gain a worldwide reputation for 'getting the job done.'

Anti-sub Helicopters?

In late 1957 the Navy made known a requirement for a new helicopter which would combine the anti-submarine hunter-killer roles. Developed with fixed-wing aircraft in World War II and carried on by pairs of helicopters post-war, it was estimated this primary task would be far more effective if one aircraft could find and attack subs.

The specification included a good weapons capability and Sikorsky's YHSS-2 proposal made its maiden flight 11 March 1959.

Considerably larger than the helo it was to supercede, the Seabat/Seahorse, the Sea King incorporated a watertight hull with outrigger stabilising floats which enclosed wheels. Power was derived from two GE T58 turboshafts driving a five-blade main rotor which had a Hamilton Standard auto-stabilization system.

Search equipment included a Bendix AQS-10 or -13 sonar fitted with a coupler to maintain hovering altitude automatically in conjunction with the Ryan APN-130 Doppler and a radar altimeter. Provision was made for up to 840 lb of homing torpedoes, depth bombs and other stores.

The Sea King, now designated the SH-3, entered service in September 1961 with VHS-10 and VHS-3 and 255 SH-3A models were delivered before introduction of the SH-3D with increased power from uprated T58 en-

Right: During the long series of manned moon shots the standard recovery procedure for astronauts was to drop the capsule in the vicinity of a carrier task force for helicopter recovery. This Sea King from HS-4 was photographed carrying out such a sortie.

Opposite: An SH-3A Sea King of Helicopter Anti-Submarine Squadron Six makes Pacific rotor wash with a sonar dunk during June 1976.

gines of 1,400 shp each. More fuel was also carried and the Navy acquired 73 examples.

On 6 March 1965, an SH-3A made the first non-stop flight across the North American continent and established a new straight-line distance record of 2166 miles. Lifting off from the deck of the USS *Hornet* moored at San Diego, California, the Sea King completed its flight by landing on the carrier *Franklin D Roosevelt* at Jacksonville, Florida.

It was also the SH-3A that made the Sea King's debut in combat when HS-6 arrived aboard the ASW carrier *Kearsarge* during 1966. With five aircraft modified by the removal of sonar gear and with armor protection for the engines, transmission and crew seats plus a 7.62 mm MG for the door gunner, this unit was soon in the rescue business; the Sea King proved to be ideal for combat SAR, particularly at night when the hover coupler intended for sonar dunking was utilised.

But the Sea King was deployed aboard the majority of US carriers stationed in the Gulf of Tonkin and these standard utility/planeguard helos occasionally became involved in rescues in the war zone. Some pre-dated the SH-3A's armed missions, although the end-product was exactly the same – the rescue of aircrews who had fallen victim to intense enemy AAA defenses.

At the height of the Vietnam War nine SH-3As were converted to mine counter-measures duties as RH-3As. Operated from

Above: When combat rescue became even more hazardous in Vietnam, the Air Force applied tactical camouflage to give some degree of protection. Since then 'low viz' schemes have remained in vogue, as this HH-3E example shows.

ships and shore bases, these helos had no AS equipment. Among the other versions of the Sea King operated by US maritime forces was the HH-3F. Based on the USAF CH-3C Jolly Green Giant of Vietnam War fame, a small number was ordered for the US Coast Guard.

The military has historically provided transportation for the President and other VIPs and the Sea King remains an important part of the inventory of this highly efficient and prestigious helicopter unit. A duty shared between the Marines and the Air Force, the former's contribution was boosted by eight specially equipped VH-3As. Operated by the Executive Flight Detachment, these aircraft were replaced in 1975 by 11 VH-3Ds with uprated engines.

A further modification program for the Sea King resulted in the HH-3A intended primarily for SAR in combat areas. A dozen machines were fitted with uprated T58-GE-8F engines, the High-Drink refuelling system with high-speed refuelling hoist and a fuel-dumping system. Provision was also made for the carriage of long-range fuel tanks.

Every HH-3A also had a 7.62 mm Minigun built into the rear of each sponson and fired by remote control by a crewman. Extra armor protection was added to shield vital areas. The HH-3A which was operated by HC-7 lent most of its features to the SH-3G which did not have an armament fit. This version was another modification program for the SH-3A and 105 examples were modified, mainly for the ASW role. This airframe, unlike the HH-3A, was based on the original Sea King without the longer fuselage and rear loading ramp and door.

In 1972 the final variant based on the SH-3A, designated SH-3H, was the subject of a big updating program. This enabled the Navy to more or less standardise on equipment for 14 squadrons (including four in the Reserve) until such time as a more modern replacement was available. Although not scheduled for replace-

ment until well into the 1990s, the Sea King and its derivatives have now been largely replaced.

LAMPS Seasprite

Shortly before the end of US involvement in Vietnam, the Navy issued a requirement for a Light Airborne Multi-Purpose System (LAMPS) to provide over-the-horizon search and strike capability for ASW destroyers. The requirement was met by an updated version of the

Below: Sceptics said it couldn't be done, that the helo would be torn apart by slipstream. Sikorsky, the Air Force and the HH-3 proved them wrong. Long range rescue thus became a reaity when this kind of operation became routine.

Opposite: A Seasprite deploying a sonobuoy.

Below: Navy Sea Stallions in contemporary camouflage.

Kaman H-2 which thus configured became the SH-2D. Among the changes was search radar set into a radome under the helicopter's nose, AS missile defence (ASMD) which included electronic jammers and more offensive punch in the form of two Mk 46/50 lightweight torpedoes. The aircraft also carries sonobuoys and is vectored into position to engage submarines located by sonar contact. LAMPS reflected a need to put ASW helicopters aboard all suitable vessels in the US fleet and after the initial batch of ten machines had been ordered, the Navy firmed up on a modification program for all 117 Seasprites then in inventory. The first SH-2F flew on 16 March 1971 and HC-4 at Lakehurst, New Jersey, was the first unit to operate it. The SH-2F deployed to sea abroad USS *Belknap* in December.

After 20 had been delivered it was decided to further improve the type with an improved rotor and avionics and greater gross weight, to 13,300 lb. The tailwheel was also located farther forward than on earlier versions. The size of the LAMPS Seasprite order justified the opening of a new production line at Kaman's New England plant and during the 1970s further refinements led to the SH-2G with two T700-GE-401 engines.

The G model remains the latest of the Seasprite line and has extended to rebuilds of the earlier UH-2A. In a program that is expected to be completed by 1990, the SH-2G is less numerous than might be supposed in 1988, with the Navy operating 50 F models and with fewer than ten G models, while the Navy Reserve was due to receive conversions of its 36 SH-2Fs. In part the Seasprite updating was to make good any capability shortfall due to late delivery of the SH-60B Seahawk – but with this now picking up (the Navy had by late 1988 at least 116 Seahawks on order) it is possible that not all the Seasprite conversions will be made.

Jolly Greens

Opposite: Air rescue in hostile jungle was not the intended duty of 'Pedro', the Kaman HH-43 Huskie. But when little else was available in Vietnam this odd little helo coped valiantly. In this view a Huskie lowers a paramedic to tend the wounded.

It was the Air Force which gave the Sikorsky HH-3E its distinctive nickname and from which this chapter takes its title – or at any rate the men on the ground awaiting rescue, to whom a big fat Sikorsky helicopter seemed the most beautiful sight in the world. The giant was in fact the symbol of a well-known brand of canned sweetcorn and one line of the accompanying jingle ran 'Down in the valley of the jolly green giant'. The name seemed appropriate for the predominantly green camouflaged choppers, and stuck.

But for the Air Force, rescue of downed flyers in Vietnam was something of a problem until 6 July 1965 when two CH-3Cs arrived at Nakhon Phanom Royal Thai Air Force Base to initiate a new era in search and rescue. Until that time, the USAF had had to rely on the trusty but short-ranged Kaman HH-43F Huskie, more popularly known as 'Pedro'. The standard Air Force rescue helicopter during the early days of the Vietnam War, the Huskie found itself undertaking missions over hostile territory, a task for which it was never designed. Unarmed and vulnerable it nevertheless served well until something more powerful could be deployed, at least in the helicopter role – for air rescue by rotary winged aircraft was still relatively new in the early 1960s. The

Air Force ordered the H-43A beginning in November 1958, 18 aircraft covering the initial order.

The slow growth of military aviation in South East Asia tended to mitigate against an organised air rescue organisation, USAF chiefs shying away from any publicity over such an element. Not unreasonably it was assumed that anyone knowing that a rescue force was in place would know that American pilots were the ones that needed rescuing – and if they were being shot down, they were flying combat missions. For a time the covert nature of air operations in the theater prevailed but after a number of fatalities among US airmen and some well-intentioned rescues by regular forces which went disasterously wrong because pilots thought that rescuing downed airmen presented no special challenges, the Air Force had little choice but to provide trained people to do the job.

The problem was equipment. Fixed-wing aircraft, including Albatross amphibians, could cope if crash survivors were in accessible terrain – but it was the mountain and jungle crashes that presented difficulties. Only helicopters would have a chance of saving men unfortunate to come down in such hostile areas.

Above: Navy helo crews' training includes MAD flights; trailing appropriate gear to locate magnetic anomolies beneath the waves, the presence of the submarine quarry can be precisely pinpointed.

ARS by Civilians

So it was that between the time that the first USAF aircraft was lost in Vietnam on 2 February 1962 and the arrival of two HH-43Bs at Nakhon Phanom on 20 June 1964 the Air Rescue Service (ARS) relied on the helicopter assets of such agencies as Air America, Continental Air Service and Bird and Son, civilian organisations that often had capacity available. Army and Marine helos were often called in on an 'as required' basis. The ARS did have its own sizeable rotary winged force, but few other than the Huskies could be spared for duty in Asia.

With their P&W R-1340-48 piston engines the original Huskies had given way to the Lycoming T53-L-1A shaft turbine in the B model to give a maximum speed of 120 mph and a range of 235 st miles. While not able to reach downed crews beyond their limited range, the Pedros were put to good use. Others followed the first two and after the Gulf of Tonkin incident put US air operations on an 'official' footing the ARS made plans to offer a more reliable service to American aircrews. The helicopter able to do so was in inventory in Tactical Air Command back in the US. Sikorsky had been judged the winner of a competition to find a long-range 'rotary winged support system' for the Air Force in July 1963.

Having obtained six SH-3As from the Navy and redesignated them SH-3Bs after the 1962 designation changes (the first three Sea Kings having been obtained in April 1962 under the original Sea King designation of HSS-2s) the USAF specified significant changes to its own version under the designation CH-3C. An entirely new cabin with extra windows and a starboard cargo door were married to a new slim rear fuselage which extended aft of a full-width cargo ramp at the rear of the cabin. Lateral sponsons into which the wheels retracted replaced the wheel outrigger pods of the SH-3 and a nosewheel gave the CH-3C a true tricycle landing gear in comparison with the tailwheel arrangement of the Sea King. In its new form the CH-3C was able to lift up to 5,000 lb internally, accommodate up to 30 troops or 15 litter cases, and had a crew of four – two pilots and two radio operators.

An Impressive Newcomer

The impressively large newcomer was a boon to the Air Rescue Service in Vietnam and despite modest numbers soon made itself felt. Arriving in Thailand on 6 July 1965 the first two Jolly Greens were followed by six more – but these latter were more suited to their new surroundings for they were HH-3Es, the first of the line to be armed.

It was an engine change that warranted redesignation of the CH-3C to -3E when 1,500 shp T58-GE-5s were fitted in February 1966. The previous month the Air Rescue Service changed its name to Aerospace Rescue and Recovery Service. The first delivery of two machines was to Vietnam, made on 10 November 1965. A much more capable rescue helo than its earlier stablemate, the HH-3E had a top speed of more than 160 mph at 7,000 ft and a ceiling of 12,000 ft, well out of range of enemy small-arms fire.

To give it range enough to reach outlying areas from bases in Thailand the HH-3E had its fuel load augmented by a pair of Super Sabre-type drop tanks attached to the landing wheel sponsons. These tanks gave an extra 400 miles which together with the larger 650-gal internal tank, enabled the type of attain a combat range of 500 miles.

Crew and passenger protection was achieved by 1,000 lb of titanium armor distributed throughout the airframe. The cockpit canopy was shatter-proof and the engines had icing and FOD protection. To assist rescues in jungles where the helo could not get near the ground, a hoist with a 240-ft cable and able to lift up to 600 lb was also fitted.

With its gradually expanding helicopter force the ARRS distributed its aircraft and crews as detachments to various bases in Thailand and South Vietnam, backing these with fixed-wing assets plus the faithful HH-43. By the summer of 1966 the USAF had a viable rescue service in the combat zone and for the remainder of the war many dramatic and hazardous flights were made, primarily to get airmen out of the clutches of their would-be captors.

Comforting the Jolly Green Giant

To ensure that their wily enemy had the least possible chance to beat the rescue teams, Jolly Green Giant missions were invariably comforted by A-1 Skyraiders, known like the Jolly Greens, by their call-sign, Sandy. The second most welcome sight to the Jolly Green to shot-down crewmen was the venerable Sandys, or Spads as the Navy called them due to their vintage, screaming down along bordering treelines to release a deadly rain of fire and shell on attacking NVA/VC forces. One of the most effective ground-attack aircraft of all time, the A-1s often made the difference between rescue or capture, but the price was high.

To extend their range until the ARRS could send its helicopters to any part of North or South Vietnam, Sikorsy, working with reports from the war zone, set about improving the

HH-3E and fitting an in-flight refuelling system. Perfecting this took time and it was not before 14 December 1966 that the first refuelling of an airborne helo took place. The tanker aircraft was a C-130 Hercules, the workhorse of the USAF, large enough to carry the fuel tanks, pumps and necessary drogues, the aerial tracking and homing equipment to guide the choppers to their aerial filling station, and the crews who would operate the transfer. Added to all this was the need to pack the Hercules with rescue and survival gear, including life rafts, flares and first aid kits.

Rescue Hercules became HC-130Ps and by the end of 1966 Lockheed had modified six aircraft. Some six months later the first HH-3E was refuelled by a C-130 in Vietnam, a concept proven in the face of some scepticism by the H-3 Systems Project Office at Wright Patterson AFB. These Air Force and civilian engineers, using a borrowed Marine Corps KC-130 tanker and a USAF H-3 worked out that instead of being torn to pieces by the propwash of the big transport, the chopper could 'ride' the slipstream in much the same manner as a boat on water, assisted by its hull design. On 17 December 1965 the Hercules took off from Cherry Point, North Carolina, for a rendezvous over the ocean. It was not inteded to make a fuel transfer but Mr James Eastman, flying the chopper would, it was hoped, carry out a 'dry' contact with one of the tanker's drogues.

Right: An early CH-53 shows its paces. Ordered for the Marines, it became an indispensable asset to the Air Force Rescue Service.

Eastman settled the H-3 on the C-130's prop-wash and it rode, just as predicted. And when the makeshift probe on the chopper's nose clunked home, a new era in military aviation was born – the traditionally short-ranged helicopter could now fly anywhere.

Following some more demonstrations of the technique, including a well-publicised flight across the Atlantic for the 1967 Paris Air Show by two HH-3Es and five HC-130Ps, Sikorsky initiated a modification program to give the Jolly Greens the refuelling gear as a standard fit. The trans-Atlantic flight involved eight re-fuellings although only one of the Hercules made the flight the whole way, a total distance of 4,157 miles. By so doing the American team set a number of helicopter records including those for speed – the HH-3Es averaged

Below: A CH-3 gets a fill-up during Exercise Jack Frost in 1979. In this, as in most other cases, the tanker is a C-130.

131 mph throughout – distance and endurance.

This new flexibility highlighted the need for a C-130 to become an integral part of the air-refuelling team – not solely as a tanker but a 'command and control' ship or aerial rescue command post to coordinate mission planning en route to the pick-up area, during the rescue, and to cover the egress and the flight back to base. A further advantage of air refuelable helos was there was often a need, particularly in mountainous terrain, for the choppers to dump fuel. Previously impossible because fuel reserves could have dropped dangerously low, helicopters could now dump fuel at any time, make the pick-up and exit the area to head for the nearest tanker. It was a very significant advantage and one that revolutionised air rescue.

One more element was always necessary for the ARRS to function smoothly, and that was highly trained, dedicated personnel. During the rescue the man on the ground often needed assistance, either because he was wounded, unable to exercise free movement due to being tangled in parachute shroud lines, or pinned down by the enemy. Any or all of these situations was the province of the pararescue man, whose job it was to see that, come what many, the helicopter would leave the area with the person or persons it had come to get.

Regularly laying their lives on the line to get the job done, pararescuemen or parajumpers, as they are also known, were the most decorated Air Force personnel of the war. Each one was a scuba diver, medical technician and parachutist, equally able to survive in conditions ranging from jungle to desert, arctic to swampland and to defend himself and his 'customers' through his expertise with small arms and in hand-to-hand combat. It was the parajumper who was the most exposed to enemy fire as he stood in the doorway of the helicopter to manoeuver a Stokes litter for the men on the ground, or who swung down on the hoist cable to give a helping hand. Only when the last man was aboard would the parajumper take his place in the chopper – if there was room On occasion, it was he who was left behind to await rescue by another helo once the wounded had been taken out.

That rescue work was tough, demanding tough aircraft and methods, was hardly in doubt – and certainly not in Vietnam. Rescue craft became prime targets for enemy gunners and there was every necessity to have the ability to shoot their way out of a hot situation. Fixed wing escorts did the job as best they could but they could not fully cover the helicopter, particularly during a lengthy rescue operation. Firepower directed by the helo crew was the only way to deal with a really close threat.

Although the Air Force explored the possibility of acquiring a new, highly specialised and very fast combat rescue aircraft, it was realised that the gestation period for a completely new aircraft would be prohibitive. The H-3 was provided with a 7.62 mm MG for self-defense but this proved to be far lighter than what was required. A heavier, roomier helicopter more able to absorb battle damage and mount its own heavier weapons, was needed. Fortunately Sikorsky had met an order from the Marines for a heavy lift helicopter in August 1962, and this machine it was estimated would be ideal in giving the ARRS more mucle.

Field Heavy Lift

While the Air Force found a gap in its inventory for a heavy lift helicopter for a specialised purpose, the Army had foreseen the need for such a machine as part of its 1950s airmobility experiments. In a move which also aimed at standardising its transport helicopters in the heavy cargo – 16 to 22 tons – class, the Army ordered the Boeing Vertol Chinook in June 1959. With a crew of three and accommodation for up to 44 troops or 24 litters the HC-1A, as it was originally designated, had a maximum permissible weight of 46,000 lb, including a payload of over 25,000 lb in later models.

By far and away one of the most important helicopters ever to enter service with the Army the CH-47 (which it became in 1962) the Chinook offered unprecedented lifting capa-bility. Similar in configuration to the smaller H-46 Sea Knight from which it inherited much Boeing Vertol experience with large turbine-powered helicopters, the Chinook gradually replaced elderly piston-engined types such as the H-37 Mojave. Production deliveries to the Army began in August 1962 with the CH-47A.

The first Chinooks arrived in Vietnam in September 1965 to operate with the 1st Cavalry Division (Airmobile) from An Khe. Other units were equipped and the mighty CH-47 soon made its presence felt. Two years on the Chinook was returning the kind of operating figures widely reflected by other types which flew day in day out on a host of duties from liaison to ammunition and weapons lifts: over 238,000 sorties to move 610,000 tons of cargo and 671,000 passengers in over 88,000 flight hours.

In that 24-month period each Chinook had averaged more than 44 hours per month and, as well as transporting people and cargo in and out of the various combat areas, the type had proven itself a great guardian of the US taxpayers' money by retrieving over 1,350 downed aircraft from the battlefield.

Arduous 'hot and high' conditions were however very tough on aircraft systems, electronics and engine reliability and the Chinook was not alone in finding Vietnam's hostile environment a factor in reducing performance and in turn, payload. Added to this was the need for the machine to carry some

Left: Slung loads have increased the usefulness of numerous helicopters, among them the Chinook. This one demonstrates the ease with which a 155mm howitzer can be lifted, while the gun's 11-man crew ride in the cabin. With 32 rounds of ammo, the M198 and its crew weigh 22,000 lb.

The increasing use of ground-to-air missiles has led to a great need for updating to increase survivability of helicopters which were designed to older, less demanding specifications. This CH-47D shows typical modern configuration and paint scheme.

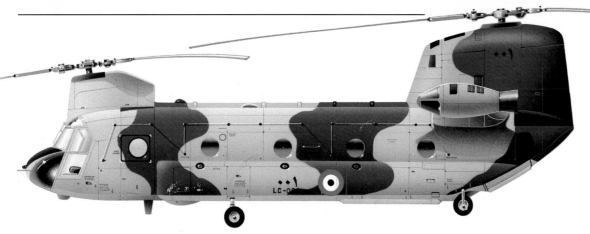

Below: Longevity personified is this CH-47B updated to Delta standard after 3,160 flight hours and SE Asian combat. Under the Initial Operational Capability (IOC) program, hundreds of older Chinooks are getting a new lease of life.

Above: World sales of US helicopters have been extensive ever since the industry became established. This Chinook is an example sold to Egypt, a nation that also operates Russian and European helicopters.

self-protective firepower, an extra crewman to act as a gunner, and some armor plating to shield vital areas of the aircraft itself as well as the crew.

The Chinook's Problems

It soon became apparent that for Vietnam war conditions, the A model Chinook needed a power boost and even before 1965 was out the 1st Cavalry made it known that an improvement in hot weather performance was urgently needed. This was only one item in a list of problems that had been revealed under combat conditions and although field maintenance teams overcame many of them, an improved aircraft was the real answer. Boeing Vertol responded well and on 10 May 1967 delivered the first CH-47B.

Able to carry more fuel for its 3,750 shp T55 engines (compared with the 2,650 shp offered by the CH-47A's T55-L-7C engines) the B model was very welcome, particularly to Army artillery teams which were invariably required to provide fire support for the numerous, often small-scale, assaults on the enemy throughout South Vietnam. A Chinook was quite capable of air lifting an entire 105 mm howitzer battery, its gun crews and ammunition from one location to another in just 11 sorties. This gave the advantage of having fire support brought into areas well beyond the range of prepared artillery positions.

Chinooks were invaluable in supporting the many 'fire bases' established by the Army; these bases, often very small, could nevertheless be swarming with combat engineers after a CH-47 lift. And if the base was too small for the helo to put down the Chinook became a relatively stable, hovering platform for troops to simply walk out onto the ramp and down ladders dangling out the back. The engineers could then use their equipment to construct a helicopter landing pad for heavier equipment to be brought in. Exemplifying the term 'airmobility' to its fullest extent, the CH-47 became a true workhorse, able as it was to ply the newly constructed base with a vast array of material including bulldozers to clear undergrowth, all in a matter of hours. If required, equipment would also be brought in to dig foxholes and trenches – no longer did the combat soldier have to undertake such chores. The Chinook became a sort of rotary-winged Skytrain, it being a neat coincidence that its numerical designation was the same as the Douglas transport which had won undying fame in World War II and Korea for similar fixed-wing duty and was, of course, still serving in SE Asia.

When it came to recovering downed aircraft, the CH-47 could lift one on its own, although a Chinook was more easily lifted by the CH-54 Skycrane which was designed to carry a ten-ton payload. Again the 1st Cavalry was the first unit to operate the Skycrane in Vietnam.

A highly specialised machine, the CH-54 was a pure cargo helicopter unable to carry any form of defensive weapon. It had therefore to be used only in non-contested areas – but its usefulness was not lessened by that fact. Able to lift items such as the M-114A1 155 mm howitzer without the need to disassemble, as was necessary for carriage by Chinook, the Skycrane's muscle often proved to be worth every cent of the $2.2 million that each one cost. Although not offensive in the accepted sense, the CH-54 did become a 'heavy bomber' in the course of its Vietnam service. Carrying a 10,000 lb M-121 bomb with extended fuse, a single Skycrane could create an 'instant landing zone' in dense jungle. When the bomb detonated the fuse extender spread the blast outwards without forming a crater.

Proving that sleek lines are not everything in helicopter capability, the dramatically ugly Skycrane can lift massive, awkward loads. It clutches a custom-designed 'people pod' between its outrigger gear legs.

Limited use was also made of the 'people pod' designed for the Skycrane to carry between its landing gear legs, but the aircraft was used mostly as a transport with slung loads.

The Super Jolly

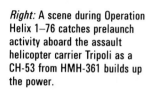

Right: A scene during Operation Helix 1–76 catches prelaunch activity aboard the assault helicopter carrier Tripoli as a CH-53 from HMH-361 builds up the power.

The urgency attending the acquisition of a larger, more powerful helicopter for the air rescue role in Vietnam was answered by the Sikorsky H-53. Ordered for the Marines in August 1962 as the CH-53A Sea Stallion, it was at that time the largest rotary-wing type in production in the West. Sikorsky drew on its experience, particularly with the CH-54, to produce a machine with a more conventional configuration. It utilised many of the Skycrane's components and was ordered by the Marines to fulfill a heavy assault role, carrying up to 55 troops.

Weighing 35,000 lb for normal take off, the Sea Stallion was a strong machine, as it was also designed to accommodate cargo. Dual doors at the rear of the fuselage incorporated a winch system to facilitate loading and off-loading of wheeled vehicles and other freight. Specified loads included a complete Honest John missile and trailer, a Hawk missile, a 105 mm howitzer and trucks up to $1\frac{1}{2}$ ton plus trailers. The spacious fuselage could be rigged for ambulance duties and was water-tight along its lower section to enable emergency landings on the sea, assisted by spon-

sons designed to accommodate the main landing gear legs.

During 1966 the USAF put in hand procurement plans for eight CH-53Bs (to distinguish this version from the USMC A model) and borrowed two examples from the Marines for crew familiarisation and training. Sikorsky meanwhile incorporated 1,200 lb of armor plate, three 7.62 mm Miniguns to fire from each side and from the rear, a retractable in-flight refuelling probe and hard points for two 450-gal US fuel tanks. Pilot ejection seats were also installed as were uprated 2,910 shp General Electric T64–GE–3 turboshaft engines and improved avionics. In this form, the Super Jolly had a range of 540 st miles at a maximum speed of 195 mph at sea level and a service ceiling of 18,550 ft.

On 19 June 1967 the ARS took delivery of the first HHO-HH-53B and on 14 September two arrived at Vung Tau for assignment to Udorn, Thailand, and the 37th ARRS's Detachment 2. To the crews, the mighty HH-53 was a BUFF – Big, Ugly Fat Fellow – although their preference for using another four-letter word rather than 'fellow' virtually forced the Air Force into slapping the name Super Jolly Green Giant on the new acquisition!

The Super Jolly with its far superior capability compared with the HH-3 soon integrated completely into ARRS mission requirements and in company with A-1 Skyraiders and Hercules tanker/command and control aircraft, rescues in Vietnam became a smoothly efficient service, often with a formidable task force engaged on the extraction of just one man from under the noses of the enemy. No effort was spared at least to try to recover shot-down aircrew and the ARRS backed its motto 'That others may live' to the hilt.

By the summer of 1969 the Air Rescue Service in Vietnam had reached a peak strength of 71 aircraft distributed among four squadrons based in Vietnam and Thailand; at any given time these units had small numbers of aircraft awaiting the call to action on nearly three times that number of landing strips near combat zones. It had been learned the hard way that a successful rescue often depended on the helicopter reaching the stranded aviator as quickly as possible and it was the increased speed and refuelling capability of the HH-53 that made the difference. It could also give a fearsome account of itself if the rescue attempt was contested by the enemy. Between 1966–70 the ARRS saved 980 aircrew from capture and a further 1,059 other lives had been saved as a result of this unique unit's efforts. As with many other techniques forged in the heat of war, the ARRS would live on afterward to become an integral part of the USAF.

New Generation

When the dust of Vietnam had finally settled for America many valuable lessons pertain-

Left: The mighty six-bladed rotor of the CH-53 appears to have a seventh in this photo, which shows the three-engined Echo version. With a take off weight of 73,000 lb the Super Stallion is the biggest helicopter in the Western world.

57

ing to operational doctrine were absorbed by the military. These were far reaching and too numerous to describe fully here – but if there was one single factor to emerge from the conflict it was that the value of the helicopter was 100 per cent proven to all four US services. Each employed different machines for a seemingly endless list of duties and post-war budgets were to reflect massive on-going procurement, not only of established types but improved models of the machines that had won their spurs in battle, and others intended for battles that might take place at some future date.

The US Army, the world's largest helicopter operator, sought an updated troop transport for the ageing Huey, and a machine specifically tailored to the role of tank killing, one that had emerged significantly at the end of the Vietnam war. Further ahead was the as-yet unproven ability of the helicopter to take on another helicopter in air-to-air combat – in 1988 this remains a role of the future.

The new aircraft for the Army would be integrated into the existing force structure, a large part of which was based on a formidable number of Bell AH-1 HueyCobras, updated and modified to the anti-armor task. On the transport side, a machine larger than the UH-1H and able to carry a greater number of troops would obviously be desirable, particularly if it had a supplementary ground attack capability. The machine chosen to fulfil this requirement was the Sikorsky UH-60 Black Hawk.

In August 1972 the Army announced its Utility Tactical Transport Aircraft System – UTTAS which is layman's terms meant a fast assault helicopter able to carry 11 fully equipped combat troops and a crew of three. Industry response resulted in a seven-month fly-off competition with Boeing Vertol's YUH-61A, at the end of which the Sikorsky contender was judged the winner. The YUH-60 made its maiden flight on 17 October 1974.

Capable of a maximum speed of 191 kts with a range of 324 miles, the UH-60 is also highly manoeuvrable for a helic... a take off weight exceed... ing a cargo lift capacity... struction utilises a n... materials and features... glassfibre/Nomex hone... which are electrically... head fitted with elastomeric bearings which need no lubrication. A comprehensive avionics suite includes radar warning – but any active role in suppressing hostile radars was left to another version, the electronic warfare EH-60B. Some A models were also modified to suit the ECM role, as EH-60As.

Far left: 'Coupla seconds more'. A crewman puts implicit trust in the pilot's ability to hold his CH-53 steady while the external load is secured to the hook.

Right: The YUH-60A made its first flight in October 1974 and led to the widely produced Black Hawk series which has been ordered by all US services. Its configuration was built around the ability to survive in 'hot' landing zones and fit inside a C-141 for long-range ferrying.

First issued to units of the 101st Airborne Division during 1979–80 the Black Hawk is generally well liked by crews and field commanders alike, although early in its career the type attracted a degree of unfavourable publicity in the US media when a number of aircraft crashed with considerable loss of life.

Having taken part in a number of exercises in order to integrate it into Army assault plans, the Black Hawk suddenly found itself in a 'real war' situation when Operation Urgent Fury took place on 20-29 October 1983. This combined operation was to secure the island of Grenada from Cuban and revolutionary elements, following a Caribbean Community States appeal for order to be restored. The call was responded to by the US which sent two separate, small task forces to land parties of SEALs and an airborne Marine assault from Sea Knight helicopters supported by Cobra gunships.

This landing was successful and Hercules transports arrived, intending to drop paratroops. This was all but aborted when heavy fire was observed although one small group who failed to hear the 'abort' order, jumped. After ground fire suppression by AC-130s the main drop was made.

The Black Hawk's debut came during the early hours of 25 October to support Delta Force troops of the 101st Airborne who were already in place having been airlifted from the USS *Guam*. Delays on the ground had enabled

Left: A quartet of Black Hawks sweep past an Army command post during an exercise. Well proven in such war rehearsals, the UH-60 has also had its baptism of fire in Grenada.

Above: The HH-60A Night Hawk has been developed for the combat SAR role and covert Special Forces missions.

Left: Able to refuel in flight, the HH-60A also carries extra fuel tanks on shoulder mounted pylons, keeping the fuselage sides clear.

AA defences to resist the helo assault and one UH-60 was shot down. The mission was abandoned.

The following day the 82nd Airborne arrived on the island and had their UH-60s air-transported to Grenada. On the third day of the operation, eight of these aircraft were prepared for a local action against a barracks complex. The helos took off and formed two flights of four, staying low to avoid ground fire. While going in to land troops in the deployment area the third helo, call sign Chalk Three, took a hit in the tail rotor, swung into Chalk Two and both sets of main rotor blades proceeded to slice each other to pieces. Trying to avoid the debris, Chalk Four made a hard landing and snapped its tail off.

the pilot could not prevent the Black Hawk flipping over onto a group of US Rangers.

The other quartet of UH-60s deployed their troops, who rapidly secured the camp area, but only two of the helos escaped damage and one limped out to the *Guam* with its crew wounded and 45 bullet holes in its fuel tanks, rotors and cabin area. Later, in an attempt to lift the damaged Black Hawks the Army requested a lift from a Marine Sea Stallion. In a small fiasco, the pilot dropped two UH-60s, totally writing both of them off.

In spite of all that, the Grenada operation was concluded successfully and although the UH-60 did not see very much action, the lion's share going to Marine CH-46 Sea Knight and Cobra gunships, it was the subject of favour-

able reports, particulary for its ruggedness under fire. Army inventory of troop transport models built up rapidly and by the winter of 1988 the number in service and on order had risen to over 800 EH/UH-60As.

Adaptation of the Black Hawk airframe to roles other than troop carrying has been fairly rapid; in Huey tradition the aircraft can defend its human cargo during a 'hot landing' with its two 7.62 mm MGs. These can be supplemented by other stores including up to 16 Hellfire laser-guided missiles – although the Army stresses that the Black Hawk does not have a primary anti-armor role. The Hellfire load is certainly formidable, but the Black Hawk does not carry its own laser target designator or

Left: The Navy has a requirement of just under 400 Seahawks for ASW and SAR roles and these are in the process of being delivered.

Below: A UH-60 demonstrates its versatility in the aerial resupply role.

sight and has to have its target identified from another source, most likely a SOTAS-equipped helo.

As mentioned, part of the Army's inventory of Black Hawks includes the EH-60A, an ECM-dedicated version with Quick Fix II Radar Warning Augmentation, Chaff flare dispenser equipment and infra-red jammer capability. The Hellfire acquisition task is being undertaken by Black Hawks fitted with the SOTAS stand-off target acquisition system which identifies and classifies moving battlefield targets under all weather conditions from a data terminal. Cabin mounted, this terminal is fed from a large rotating surveillance radar antenna under the fuselage.

The Black Hawk is an ongoing program and among the versions projected for future service with the Army are the updated UH-60B to perform much the same role as the A model, and the UH-60C which will represent a further 1990s update with uprated engines. Whether or not these models will in fact enter service is open to question; there have been hints that the new US administration under George Bush might be obliged to put some constraints on expensive helicopter programs both for the Army and the other services.

Below: In the Huey tradition, the Army uses a number of its Black Hawks for casevac/ambulance duties, the international red cross marking only slightly compromising the otherwise drab low viz markings and paintwork.

Right: Four Black Hawks traverse a lake during a training a sortie.

Apache

Taking the prize for the ugliest helicopter ever built – or the most functional, depending on your point of view, the Hughes (McDonnell Douglas) AH-64 is every inch a combat helicopter. With the entire airframe given over to getting its two-man crew and formidable armament into position on the battlefield, the Apache's primary mission is to knock out tanks.

Development of the Apache also began in 1972 when the Army, looking again at the old AAFSS requirement that had been partially met by the HueyCobra, realised that the more immediate requirement was for an advanced Attack Helicopter (AAH). Both Bell with the YAH-63 and Hughes Helicopters, offering the YAH-64, were invited to build competitive prototypes.

Neither design was anything like the AAFSS winner, the Lockheed Cheyenne, nor indeed

Far right: Not the most handsome machine ever to hang under a rotor, the Apache nevertheless has an angular appeal. Most importantly, it is a very potent attack helicopter.

Right: Tests continue to make modern helicopters able to take on other helos in an air-to-air dual. Here, the AH-64 launches an AIM-9M Sidewinder heat seeking missile over the White Sands range.

Right: Systems redundancy enables the AH-64 to withstand hits by any type of ammunition up to 23mm caliber and in emergency, either crewman can fly it.

Far right: Should the air combat role ever materialise, the Apache is manoeuvrable enough to look after itself.

Below: The Hughes AH-64 Apache is the most sophisticated battlefield helicopter yet developed. It is shown in this profile wearing its low visability, combat camouflage.

Above: Carrying a mix of Rockwell Hellfire and conventional folding fin rockets in pods, two AH-64As leap a Texas river and head for the range.

were submissions from Boeing Vertol, Sikorsky – and Lockheed. Hughes was judged the winner of the competition in December 1976, the Army being impressed with the degree of protection afforded by the ungainly looking aircraft, its reduced IR signature and its ability to incorporate a degree of electronic and IR counter-measures equipment.

The design of the Apache was undoubtedly influenced by the strides made in helicopter gunships by the Soviet Union. By the late 1960s from modest beginnings the Russians had advanced into the potent Mil-24, a helicopter which was in turn influenced by the potential of the US AAFSS program. Among other roles, the Mi-24 (NATO codename Hind) was deemed a useful aircraft to patrol and protect remote areas bordering China following Sino-Soviet skirmishes during the 1960s.

Although long range was not of paramount importance, the Apache is able to cross the Atlantic under its own power (there is no in-flight refuelling capability) if it carries the maximum amount of external fuel in sponson-mounted drop tanks. Normal range is 330 nm.

The first flight of the YAH-64 took place on 30 September 1975 but it would be just a over a decade before the production version was declared to be operational. The long gestation period was occupied with ground and flight testing of all elements of the system and in the end, although it had a long wait, the Army got a lot more helicopter than it had originally specified.

The first changes were made to the tail. Orginally having a tall fin with a 'T' stabiliser, a curved-section cockpit canopy and smoothly rounded nose, the first Air Vehicles (pre-production prototypes), were modified to accommodate the 'sharp edged' features with which the Apache was to enter Army service.

The old canopy gave way to a huge, flat-panelled glasshouse stepped down to afford the pilot, in the second tandem seat, a degree of forward view over the co-pilot/gunner's position up front. The extreme snout now held a sensor for target acquisition, and the tailfin was completely redesigned with the previously mid-mounted tail rotor repositioned at

Left: You need plenty of space to realistically test combat helicopters and crew proficiency and luckily the US has an abundance of acres in which to play at war. This Apache is passing features which would have been familiar to its Indian namesake of a century ago.

the top. The horizontal stabiliser was moved to the base of the fin, immediately above the tailwheel.

Armament tests covered a variety of air-to-ground weapons including the trusty 2.75 in folding-fin aircraft rocket (FFAR) in 19-round pods, eight TOW missiles in two quadruple launchers and Hughes' own XM230 Chain Gun.

This latter is the helo's primary area weapon, and has second-to-none reliability. A 1976 Department of Defense directive specified that the 30 mm weapon be adapted to take Nato ammunition as well as three basic types of US round – high explosive, practise and dual-purpose HE. Commonality with Nato ammo was important as Europe has to be a primary

Far right: Apache war party of AH-64As flying nap-of-the earth, their happy hunting grounds lacking nothing but European-type weather for added realism – for their tank enemy will definitely not be down in the cactus.

Right: Artist's eye view of what is probably the ultimate role for a combat helicopter – the ability to bring down another of its kind in one-on-one air-to-air combat. This is what McDonnell and other manufacturers are working up to.

threat area for any future combat involving US helicopters and a large number of tanks. The current Apache deployments to Army units in Germany reflect this possibility.

The M230 is a single-barrel weapon externally powered by a 6.5 h motor and has a rotating bolt mechanism driven by a chain. This system greatly simplifies the firing cycle and does away with the need for fairings, turret housings and any form of powered ammunition feeds or boosters. Neither does the chain gun need chargers, declutching feeders or other special devices, all of which add weight in a more conventional weapon. In two years of tests the Army fired 2,500 rounds of ammunition from various Chain Guns which differed in detail, and the results were very encouraging; rate of fire is extremely flexible, from single shot up to 625 rpm.

Hellfire

Among the things that appealed to Army top brass about the AH-64 is its ability to remain on active duty around the clock. The reliability of the aircraft is said to be such that whereas with older helicopter gunships the cycle time was about ten hours before they needed overhaul – which could last a similar time – the Apache keeps on going. Stand-down time is said to be so low that it is the human factor that sets limits rather than the machine. Men get tired; the Apache does not.

As well as the Hughes TOW missile, the

Its laser eye swivelling toward
the camera, an AH-64A peels
away for another simulated
ground attack.

Apache's armory extends to the sohisticated Rockwell Hellfire which, unlike TOW, does not need the crew to be exposed to defensive fire. To obtain an accurate hit with TOW, the wire-guidance system requires the parent helo to fly toward the target for up to 14 seconds in order that the steering signals from the CPG can continue to be transmitted 'down the wire'. Acceptable in a low-threat environment, TOW might just prove prohibitively costly in terms of men and machines when the enemy is firing back. Hellfire removes that risk.

Propelled toward the target by a solid fuel rocket motor, Hellfire reaches supersonic speed (about Mach 1.17) making it the fastest Western AT missile extant. Short flight time cuts target evasion time and enables the helo to clear the area quickly. There is no need for the launch helicopter crew to see the target at all. Using its laser designator to acquire the target, an Apache could launch several missiles in quick succession, leaving Hellfire to strike, then move safely out of range of return fire. Providing that Hellfire can always 'see' the target, it offers the advantage of climbing to a high altitude and then diving to hit what is often the weakest point of an armored vehicle – the roof. The laser designator need not be the Apache's own: another helo or a ground unit can provide the homing 'beam'. Remote designation of the target enables the attacking helicopter to remain 'hull down' throughout

the engagement – small wonder that anyone associated with modern battlefield tactics is impressed by Hellfire, a missile which in tests has returned no fewer than 100 per cent hits under all conditions by both night and day.

On 6 January 1984, shortly before Hughes became part of McDonnell Douglas, the first Apache Production Vehicle 01 (PV01) was rolled out at Mesa, Arizona. Some eight months later the Secretary of Defense was

Above: Army Apache crews at Fort Hood in Texas prepare to mount up. Missions are carefully planned so that fatigue does not reduce human effectiveness at the controls, for the Apache is a strong beast well able to fly all day without malfunction.

approving the last of 675 AH-64s for US Army service around the world. This massive program will of course see the aircraft in service throughout the 1990s and probably well beyond. The plan is to have 34 attack battalions armed with 614 Apaches by 1990.

The late 1980s/early 1990s will also see some changes in the Apache's capability, but they may not be readily apparent from outside the cockpit. There is currently great enthusiasm for low-radar signature, stealth-type materials and design work is now underway to incorporate advanced technology materials as cheaper and lighter 'secondary structure' components.

Such advances will be fitted initially in the next version, the AH-64B. As cockpit systems advance these too will be incorporated in the Apache and other contemporary US military helicopters. Recent advances now in service are TADS (Target Acquisition and Data System) and PNVS (Pilot's Night Vision System) – and around the corner are the composite materials mentioned above the new 'adaptability' in the form of non-US engines such as the R-R Turbomeca RTM 322 and the Stinger AAM for self defense.

At least the ship's aerobatic qualities give Apache crews the chance to break the routine and really wring it out for that future 'ACM' role.

US helicopters by popular name 1945-date

Name	Designation	Service	Manufacturer
Aeroscout	OH-58	Army	Bell
Apache	AH-64	Army	Hughes/McDonnell Douglas
Army Mule	H-25/HUP-2	Army/Navy	Piasecki/Vertol
Blackhawk	S-66	—	Sikorsky
Black Hawk	UH-60	Army	Sikorsky
Cayuse	OH-6	Army	Hughes/McDonnell Douglas
Cheyenne	AH-56	—	Lockheed
Chickasaw	H-19	USAF/Army	Sikorsky
Chinook	CH-47	Army	Boeing Vertol
Choctaw	H-34	Army	Sikorsky
Cobra	AH-1G/O/S	Army	Bell
Enchanced Cobra	AH-1S	Army	Bell
Huey	UH-1/HU-1 TH-1	Army/Navy USAF/Marines	Bell
HueyCobra	AH-1G	Army/Marines	Bell
Huskie	HH-43/HOK-1 UH-43/OH-43	USAF/Navy	Kaman
Improved SeaCobra	AH-1	Marines	Bell
Iroquois	UH-1 Series	Army/Navy/ USAF/Marines	Bell
Jolly Green Giant	HH-3	USAF	Sikorsky
KingCobra	Model 309	—	Bell
Kiowa	OH-58	Army	Bell
Modified Cobra	AH-1S	Army	Bell
Mojave	H-37/HR2S-1	Army/Marines Navy	Sikorsky
Night Hawk	HH-60	—	Sikorsky
Oceanhawk	SH-60	—	Sikorsky
Osage	H-55	Army	Hughes
Pelican	CH-3	—	Sikorsky
Quick Hawk	EH-60	Army	Sikorsky
Raven	HTE-1/H-23	Navy/Army	Hiller
Retriever	HUP-2	Navy	Piasecki
Seabat	HSS-1	Navy	Sikorsky
SeaCobra	AH-1J	Marines	Bell
Sea Dragon	MH-53	Navy	Sikorksy
Sea Guard	HH-52	USCG	Sikorksy
Sea Hawk	SH-60	Navy	Sikorsky
Sea Horse	HUS-1	Marines/USCG	Sikorsky
Sea King	SH-3/VH-3	Navy/Marines	Sikorsky
Sea Knight	HRB-1/H-46/ UH-46/CH-46	Navy/Marines	Boeing Vertol
Sea Ranger	H-57	Navy	Bell
Sea Sprite	HU2K/HH 2/ UH-2/H-2/SH-2	Navy	Kaman
Sea Stallion	CH-53/RH-53	Navy/Marines	Sikorsky
Shawnee	H-21/CH-21	USAF/Army	Piasecki/Vertol
Skycrane	CH-54/H-54	Army	Sikorsky
Sioux	H-13	Army/USAF	Bell
SuperCobra	AH-1W	Marines	Bell
Super Jolly (Green Giant)	HH-53	USAF	Sikorsky
Super Stallion	CH-53	Navy/Marines	Sikorsky
Tarhe	CH-54/H-54	Army	Sikorsky
Tomahawk	UH-2		Kaman
Workhorse	H-21/CH-21	USAF/Army	Piasecki/Vertol

Acknowledgements

The publishers are grateful to Jerry Scutts, aircraft manufacturers and armed forces for most of the illustrations in this book, and to Pilot Press (pages 11, 13, 24, 30, 32, 35, 36, 37, 38, 39, 42, 46, 50, 51, 56, 60, 63, 64, 65, 66, 67, 70).